Inf.

W9-AOP-964

Endangered Animals of AFRICA

SAVE EARTH'S ANIMALS!

Marie Allgor

PowerKiDS press

New York

Published in 2011 by The Rosen Publishing Group, Inc.
29 East 21st Street, New York, NY 10010

First Edition

Editor: Jennifer Way
Book Design: Julio Gil

Photo Credits: Cover, pp. 15, 22 Anup Shah/Digital Vision/Thinkstock; pp. 4, 5 (inset), 7 (top), 8, 9 iStockphoto/Thinkstock; p. 5 (top) Max Hurdebourcq/AFP/Getty Images; p. 6 Hemera/Thinkstock; pp. 7 (inset), 12, 16, 17, 18, 19 Shutterstock.com; p. 10 Tom Brakefield/Stockbyte/Thinkstock; p. 11 Jupiterimages/ Photos.com/Thinkstock; p. 13 Roger de la Harpe/Getty Images; p. 14 © Eric Miller/Peter Arnold, Inc.; p. 20 © WILDLIFE/Peter Arnold, Inc.; p. 21 DEA/G. ROLI/De Agostini/Getty Images.

Library of Congress Cataloging-in-Publication Data

Allgor, Marie.
  Endangered animals of Africa / by Marie Allgor. — 1st ed.
     p. cm. — (Save earth's animals!)
  Includes index.
  ISBN 978-1-4488-2528-8 (library binding) — ISBN 978-1-4488-2640-7 (pbk.) —
  ISBN 978-1-4488-2641-4 (6-pack)
  1. Endangered species—Africa—Juvenile literature. 2. Wildlife conservation—Africa—
Juvenile literature. I. Title.
  QL84.6.A1A584 2011
  591.68096—dc22
                                    2010022486

Manufactured in the United States of America

CPSIA Compliance Information: Batch #WW11PK: For Further Information contact Rosen Publishing, New York, New York at 1-800-237-9932

Contents

Welcome to Africa   4

Africa's Climate   6

Africa's Habitats   8

Africa's Endangered Animals   10

Danger for African Wild Dogs   12

Black Rhinos in Trouble   14

Save Geometric Tortoises!   16

Grévy's Zebras   18

Help Eurasian Peregrine Falcons   20

Save Africa's Animals!   22

Glossary   23

Index   24

Web Sites   24

Welcome to Africa

The **continent** of Africa is home to nearly 800 million people. It is also home to countless animal **species**. Some of these animals, such as driver ants, are plentiful. Other African animals are not doing as well. There are very few of them left.

Huge herds of wildebeests live in the grasslands of southern Africa.

This person is cutting down trees in Gabon, a country in Africa.

Lions live in Africa's grasslands. These big cats have lost some of their lands due to people building roads, houses, and farms.

People have taken over many places to build roads, houses, and farms. Animals that once lived in these places no longer have food or places to live. Some of them die. If enough animals in a species die, the species becomes **endangered**. This means it is in danger of disappearing from Earth completely.

Africa's Climate

Africa is Earth's second-largest continent. It has many different **climate zones**. Climate has to do with the weather a certain place has over a long time. In general, most of Africa is warm and dry. Grasslands called savannas cover 40 percent of Africa. Another 40 percent is made up of hot, dry deserts.

Africa's deserts have hot, dry climates.

These elephants are walking across a savanna. The climate in a savanna is warm but not as dry as a desert climate.

Rain forests have warm, wet climates. Rain forests have lots of different kinds of plants and animals.

Many different animal species live on this continent. If the climate where they live changes too much, these animals can become endangered.

Africa's Habitats

A habitat is the place in which plants and animals naturally live. People are destroying many of Africa's habitats. This has endangered some of Africa's animals!

One of the world's most famous desert habitats is the Sahara, in northern Africa. Horned vipers, fennec foxes, and jerboas live there. The Kalahari and Namib deserts, in the southwest, are home to animals such as jackals, gazelles, and meerkats.

The Kalahari Desert is known for meerkats, which live in large groups there.

Ring-tailed lemurs are endangered animals that live in forest habitats in Madagascar.

The central part of Africa has thick rain forests and grasslands. Monkeys, snakes, and birds live in these parts of Africa. The southern part of Africa has savannas with many large animals, such as lions, elephants, wildebeests, and zebras.

Africa's Endangered Animals

Africa is home to some amazing animals. The animals on these pages are endangered and could one day become **extinct**.

MAP KEY

- African Wild Dog
- Black Rhino
- Chimpanzee
- Grévy's Zebra
- Mountain Gorilla

Black Rhino

1. African Wild Dog

African wild dogs live in packs of up to 20 animals. Today only 3,000 to 5,500 of these animals remain in Africa.

2. Black Rhinoceros

The black rhinoceros population is spread across areas in the southern and eastern parts of Africa. There were once about 100,000 black rhinos. Now there are only 3,100 or fewer.

3. Chimpanzee

Chimpanzees live in rain forests and wet savannas. Chimpanzee numbers are dropping due to people cutting down their forest homes, taking chimps for medical studies, and from illnesses.

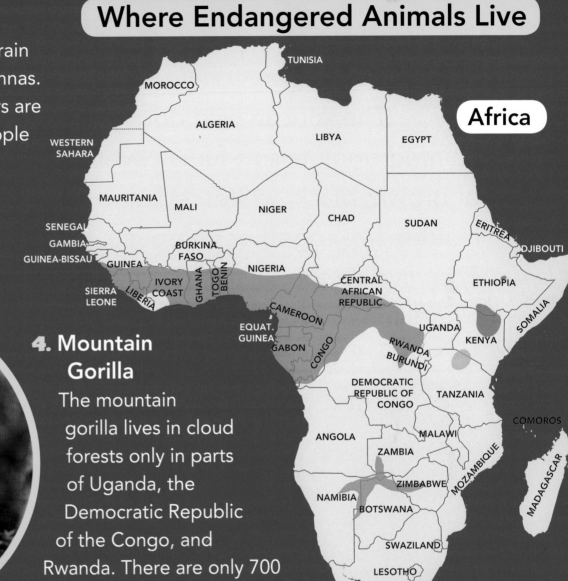

Africa

TUNISIA
MOROCCO
ALGERIA
LIBYA
EGYPT
WESTERN SAHARA
MAURITANIA
MALI
NIGER
CHAD
SUDAN
ERITREA
DJIBOUTI
SENEGAL
GAMBIA
GUINEA-BISSAU
GUINEA
BURKINA FASO
NIGERIA
CENTRAL AFRICAN REPUBLIC
ETHIOPIA
SIERRA LEONE
LIBERIA
IVORY COAST
GHANA
TOGO
BENIN
CAMEROON
SOMALIA
EQUAT. GUINEA
GABON
CONGO
UGANDA
KENYA
RWANDA
BURUNDI
DEMOCRATIC REPUBLIC OF CONGO
TANZANIA
COMOROS
ANGOLA
MALAWI
ZAMBIA
MOZAMBIQUE
MADAGASCAR
NAMIBIA
ZIMBABWE
BOTSWANA
SWAZILAND
LESOTHO
SOUTH AFRICA

Chimpanzee

4. Mountain Gorilla

The mountain gorilla lives in cloud forests only in parts of Uganda, the Democratic Republic of the Congo, and Rwanda. There are only 700 mountain gorillas alive today.

5. Grévy's Zebra

Grévy's zebra is the largest of the three zebra species. The numbers of Grévy's zebras has dropped by 83 percent since the 1970s.

11

Danger for African Wild Dogs

The African wild dog is also called the painted dog. Its soft fur is covered in spots of brown, black, white, red, and tan. These hunters live together in groups, called packs. They live on the savannas, grasslands, and open woodlands of Africa.

The African wild dog's coloring helps it blend in with the grasslands around it.

This African wild dog is looking after the pack's pups.

A mother African wild dog can give birth to as many as 16 pups in a litter, but most of these pups will die. Life is not easy for the adult dogs, either. People kill many wild dogs because they sometimes hunt livestock on farms. They are also endangered because of habitat loss and illness.

Black Rhinos in Trouble

Black rhinoceroses, or rhinos, live in an African habitat called bushveld. Bushveld is grassland that has dense **thickets**. Many of the bushes and trees in these thickets have thorns that bother other animals. They do not bother the thick-skinned rhinos, though.

Rhino horns are prized by some people. Sometimes people catch rhinos and cut off their horns so that the animals will not be killed for their horns.

Black rhinos spend most of their time by themselves.

The black rhino used to be widespread across half of Africa. There are not very many black rhinos alive in the wild today, however. One of the biggest reasons black rhinos are endangered is that people kill the black rhino for its horns. Now it is extinct in some places. People are now working hard to make sure it does not become extinct anywhere else.

Save Geometric Tortoises!

Geometric tortoises live in the southern part of South Africa. Their shells have markings, which give them their name. This shell helps the turtle keep safe.

Because of their beautiful shells, many geometric turtles were taken from the wild for the pet trade. In 1951, this practice was made unlawful. People also liked to eat the tortoise's eggs and make things out of its shell.

The markings on a geometric tortoise's shell gives it its name. Its cool-looking shell is the reason people sometimes took the tortoise from the wild to keep it as a pet. This is against the law.

The geometric tortoise is found in South Africa's Cape Province. These turtles can be found in the bushlands, such as in the Cape Point Nature Reserve, shown here.

These things are now against the law. Today the biggest problem facing the geometric tortoise is **habitat destruction**. Today there are fewer than 5,000 geometric turtles left in the world.

Grévy's Zebras

There are three kinds of zebras. They are the mountain zebra, Burchell's zebra, and the endangered Grévy's zebra. The Grévy's zebra's numbers have fallen to around 2,500.

Zebras are eaten by many of Africa's large hunters, such as lions and hyenas. People are zebras' worst enemy, though. People have hunted them for their skins and meat. People have also taken over their habitat. Zebras must compete with livestock and people for food and water.

Grévy's zebras are the largest of the three kinds of zebras. This pair of Grévy's zebras are stopping to drink water at a pond.

The stripes on a Grévy's zebra are thinner than the stripes on other zebras.

Grévy's zebras **migrate** long distances for food and water. Today they are a protected species, and it is hoped that they will come back from the edge of extinction.

Help Eurasian Peregrine Falcons

Peregrine falcons live and nest around the world, including in Africa. These birds mostly eat other birds and can even catch them in midair! Many people once hunted peregrine falcons. When the number of peregrine falcons dropped too low, laws were changed to protect the falcon from hunters.

In the 1930s and 1940s, a **pesticide** called DDT killed many peregrine falcons. At one point there were only about 600 peregrine falcons in the world. In the early 1970s,

Peregrine falcons dive out of the sky to catch their prey. This bird's dive can be as fast as 200 miles per hour (320 km/h)!

Here is a peregrine falcon in its nest with its chicks.

laws changed to control the use of DDT. Today the peregrine falcon is not endangered, but scientists pay close attention to the bird's numbers in the wild.

Save Africa's Animals!

Africa's animals need our help! Animals on the endangered list can make a comeback if people work hard to keep them safe. For example, elephants were endangered in 1996, but now their numbers are growing. This shows that **conservation** efforts work.

In Africa land is being set aside for endangered species. These **sanctuaries**, or conservation lands, help limit habitat destruction. Laws have also been passed to keep these animals safe from hunting. There are also programs to educate people about why the animals are important to Africa's **ecosystems**.

Glossary

CLIMATE ZONES (KLY-mut ZOHNZ) Large places that have the same kind of weather.

CONSERVATION (kon-sur-VAY-shun) Keeping something from being hurt.

CONTINENT (KON-tuh-nent) One of Earth's seven large landmasses.

ECOSYSTEMS (EE-koh-sis-temz) Communities of living things and the surroundings in which they live.

ENDANGERED (in-DAYN-jerd) Describing an animal whose species or group has almost all died out.

EXTINCT (ek-STINGKT) No longer existing.

HABITAT DESTRUCTION (HA-buh-tat dih-STRUK-shun) Great damage or ruin of the place where a plant or animal naturally lives.

MIGRATE (MY-grayt) To move from one place to another.

PESTICIDE (PES-tuh-syd) Poison used to kill a pest, such as an insect or rodent.

SANCTUARIES (SANK-choo-weh-reez) Protected places, or places where a living thing can be kept from being hurt.

SPECIES (SPEE-sheez) One kind of living thing. All people are one species.

THICKETS (THIH-kits) Bushes or small trees growing close together.

Index

C
climate zones, 6
continent, 4, 6–7

D
danger, 5
deserts, 6, 8

E
Earth, 5
ecosystems, 22

F
farms, 5, 13
food, 5, 18–19

G
grassland(s), 6, 9,
    12, 14

H
habitat destruction,
    17, 22
home(s), 4, 8, 11

P
people, 4–5, 8, 11,
    13, 15–16, 18,
    20, 22
pesticide, 20
plants, 8

S
sanctuaries, 22
savannas, 6, 9,
    11–12
species, 4–5, 7, 11,
    19, 22

T
thickets, 14

V
vipers, 8

Z
zebra(s), 9–11, 18–19

Web Sites

Due to the changing nature of Internet links, PowerKids Press has developed an online list of Web sites related to the subject of this book. This site is updated regularly. Please use this link to access the list:
www.powerkidslinks.com/sea/africa/